Sweeping Tsunamis

Heinemann Library
Chicago, Illinois

Louise and Richard Spilsbury

Customer Service 888-454-2279
Visit our website at www.heinemannlibrary.com

Designed by David Poole and Paul Myerscough
Originated by Dot Gradations Limited
Printed in China by WKT Company Limited

09 08 07 06 05
10 9 8 7 6 5 4 3 2 1

Library of Congress Cataloging-in-Publication Data
Spilsbury, Louise.
  Sweeping tsunamis / Louise and Richard Spilsbury.
     v. cm. -- (Awesome forces of nature)
Includes bibliographical references and index.
Contents: What is a tsunami? -- What causes a tsunami? -- Where do
tsunamis happen? -- What happens in a tsunami? -- Case study: Hawaii,
1946 -- Who helps when tsunamis happen? -- Case study: Japan, 1993 --
Can tsunamis be predicted? -- Can people prepare for tsunamis? -- Case
study: Papua New Guinea, 1998 -- Can tsunamis be prevented? --
Destructive tsunamis of the past.
  ISBN 1-4034-7275-0 (lib. bdg.) -- ISBN 1-4034-7276-9 (pbk.)
  1. Tsunamis--Juvenile literature. 2. Tsunamis--Environmental
aspects--Juvenile literature. [1. Tsunamis.] I. Spilsbury, Richard,
1963- II. Title.
  GC221.5. S69 2003
  363.34'9--dc21
                              2003001200

Acknowledgments
The author and publisher are grateful to the following for permission to reproduce copyright
material:
Cover photograph by AGE Fotostock/Imagestate.
Unlike in this picture, tsunamis rarely break as they reach the shore.

pp. 4, 28 Getty Images; pp. 5, 12, 21 Rex Features; p. 7 Charles O'Rear/Corbis; p. 9 EPA/Mike
Nelson; p. 11 Pacific Tsunamis Museum; p. 13 Mary Plage/Oxford Scientific Films; p. 14
Reuters/Enny Nuraheni; p. 15 Todd A. Gipstein/Corbis; p. 17 John Russell/Getty Images/AFP; p.
18 Scanpix Nordfoto/EPA/AFP; p. 19 Associated Press; p. 20 Jewel Samad/Getty Images/AFP;
p. 22 David Butow/Corbis; p. 23 Carlos Munoz-Yague/LDG/EURELIOS/Science Photo Library;
p. 24 Te Papa Tongarewa Museum of New Zealand; p. 25 Science Photo Library; p. 26 NOAA;
p. 27 Wolfgang Kaehler/Corbis.

Some words are shown in bold, **like this.** You can find out what
they mean by looking in the glossary.

Contents

What Is a Tsunami?

A tsunami is a huge destructive ocean wave. It is nothing like an ordinary wave. As ocean waves move into shallow water, their narrow foaming tips curl over and 'break' (collapse). A tsunami hits land as a dark, fast-moving ledge of water that rarely breaks as it nears shore. Most tsunamis are barely noticeable in deep parts of oceans, but they get bigger as they approach land.

TSUNAMI FACTS

! The biggest tsunamis are the most destructive waves on the planet.

! The fastest tsunamis in the world can reach speeds of 800 kilometres per hour.

! Tsunamis have reached heights of 40 metres above the normal level of the sea.

Big tsunamis can move toward land at hundreds of miles per hour. This photo of a first tsunami wave was taken by a tourist on the island of Penang, Malaysia, in December 2004.

Awesome force

Big tsunamis are like huge walls of water. They can be tens of feet tall and a few miles wide, containing millions of tons of water. The water smacks hard onto land with the same force as a wall of concrete.

Anything in the path of a big tsunami—from people to giant ships or trucks—may be swept away, crushed, or buried under water. Trees and telephone poles are snapped like matchsticks. Homes, schools, and lighthouses may collapse as if made of cardboard. Over the past 100 years, tsunamis have killed tens of thousands of people and caused millions of dollars' worth of damage around the world.

Harbor waves

Tsunami is a Japanese word that means "harbor wave." It was given this name because of the great devastation caused around the coastal harbors of Japan by many tsunamis.

The 2004 Indian Ocean tsunami caused flooding on Koh Racha Island in Thailand. This shows one of the three large waves that destroyed a luxury hotel.

What Causes a Tsunami?

Tsunamis usually happen when giant chunks of land at the bottom of the ocean drop down as the result of an **earthquake.** Millions of tons of seawater move in to fill the gap. This water movement causes a series of waves on the surface of the ocean—a bit like the ripples that spread out when you drop a stone into a pond or lake.

Earth movements

The outer layer of Earth is made of solid rock. On mountain tops it may be bare, on deserts it may be covered with sand, and in oceans it is covered with seawater. Incredibly, this rock is always moving, although it does so very slowly. Deep inside Earth it is so hot that the rock is melted into a sticky liquid. The cooler, lighter rock of the surface floats around on top of this liquid in enormous chunks called **plates.**

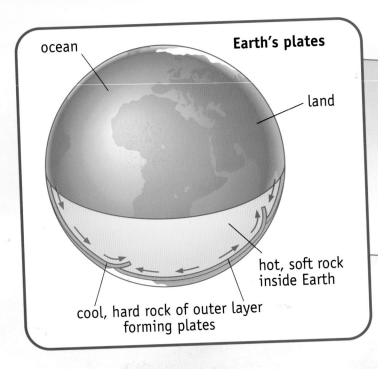

ocean

Earth's plates

land

hot, soft rock
inside Earth

cool, hard rock of outer layer
forming plates

As Earth's plates move,
they push and slide
against each other.
Sometimes the plates
stick, and then one
suddenly slips down,
causing an earthquake.

Other causes of tsunamis

All tsunamis start when massive amounts of seawater are suddenly moved. Sometimes the **lava** in Earth spurts out through gaps or thin spots in the plates. This is what we call a **volcano.** When underwater volcanoes explode, they destroy rocks around them and can start tsunamis.

Tsunamis can also be started when large amounts of rock or ice on mountains suddenly break free and fall into water. Tsunamis would also happen if a large meteorite—a piece of rock from space—plunged into an ocean.

In 1883, the Krakatoa volcano in Indonesia erupted. The whole island collapsed and caused 115-foot (35-meter) high tsunamis that sped toward neighboring islands, killing 36,000 people.

Deep beginnings

Tsunamis move outward from the point where they start. Imagine you are on a plane flying over an ocean. If an **earthquake** struck hundreds of feet under water on the **seafloor,** all you would see is crumpled water for an instant. The sea would then flatten again and a tsunami would speed away.

Tsunamis travel fastest in deep water. The **crest** of a tsunami in deep water may be only three feet (one meter) tall. This crest is just the tip of a deep wave that reaches tens of feet into the water. As the wave moves toward shallower water, the top pushes forward at a fast speed, but the bottom slows down as it touches the seafloor. The water then bunches up and the tsunami reaches its tallest height as it arrives at the coast.

Tsunamis can build to great heights as they get closer to land. Although they slow down, they can still hit coastlines at hundreds of miles per hour.

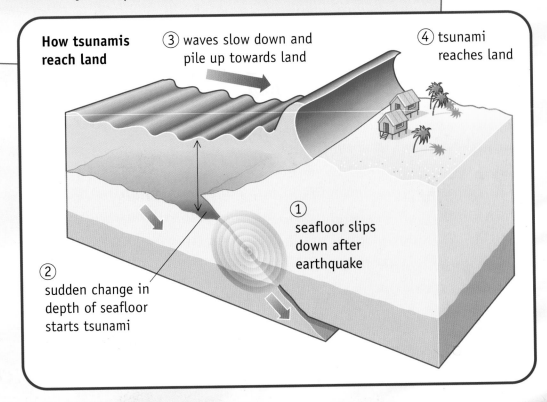

How tsunamis reach land

③ waves slow down and pile up towards land

④ tsunami reaches land

① seafloor slips down after earthquake

② sudden change in depth of seafloor starts tsunami

Enormous forces

Tsunamis shift huge quantities of water at such high speeds that they can travel very long distances. In 1960, an earthquake off Chile in South America started a tsunami. The tsunami traveled more than 9,000 miles (15,000 km) in 22 hours before hitting the coast of Japan. A big tsunami is barely slowed down when it moves over a small island, but it usually stops after it hits a **continent.** Some large tsunamis bounce off continents and move back and forth over whole oceans, getting gradually weaker over several days.

Tsunamis and tidal waves

Tsunamis are sometimes incorrectly called tidal waves. Tidal waves are waves caused by tides. Tides are the regular rise and fall of the level of the oceans, caused by the pull of **gravity** from the Moon and the Sun. Especially high tides sometimes cause large tidal waves, but never tsunamis.

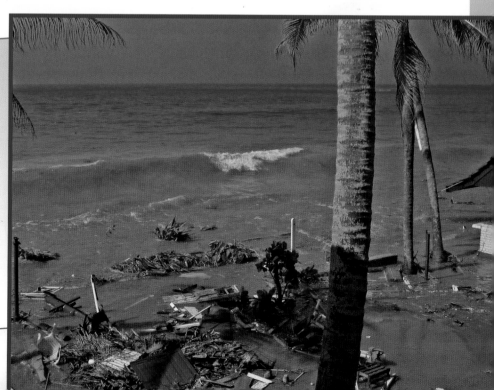

After the first tsunami waves, weaker waves continue to hit the mainland, adding to the damage. Here, the town of Hakkeduwa in Sri Lanka is being hit by the later waves of the 2004 Indian Ocean tsunami.

Where Do Tsunamis Happen?

Most tsunamis happen in the Pacific Ocean. Some of the countries most at risk from tsunamis are Japan, the United States, Papua New Guinea, and Chile, because they border the Pacific. Tsunamis happen in the Pacific Ocean because a part of Earth's outer surface, called the Pacific **plate,** lies underneath it. There are many **earthquakes** and **volcanoes** along the edges of this plate, where it meets other plates. This area is often called the "ring of fire."

Where else do they happen?

Tsunamis affect other coasts around oceans where earthquakes happen. They have hit countries in the Indian Ocean, Canada, which is at the edge of the Atlantic Ocean, and countries around the Mediterranean Sea.

The countries around the edge of the Pacific Ocean are all at risk from tsunamis. Certain Pacific islands, such as Hawaii, are at even greater risk because they are in the middle of the ring of fire. Tsunamis can approach from all sides!

The Ring of Fire

RUSSIA

Alaska (USA)

CANADA

San Francisco
USA
Los Angeles

•Tokyo
JAPAN

Hawaii
(USA)

PAPUA
NEW
GUINEA

INDONESIA

PACIFIC
OCEAN

AUSTRALIA

CHILE

NEW ZEALAND

KEY
||| ring of fire

Shape of the land

Some parts of coasts are more affected by tsunamis than others. Towns and villages in greatest danger are those at **sea level** less than 1.25 miles (2 km) from the sea. Even very small tsunamis can travel a long way over flat land.

Tsunamis are also dangerous in curved bays or at the end of **fjords.** The waves get very high between their narrow sides. When tsunamis reach a **headland**—a narrow strip of land sticking out into the sea— they wrap around it. Then water floods onto land from both sides.

TSUNAMI FACTS

! The highest tsunami ever recorded happened in 1958 in Lituya Bay, Alaska. A **landslide** fell into the narrow fjord causing a wave more than 1,600 feet (500 meters) high—that's taller than the Sears Tower!

Tsunamis can roll much farther inland over a flat coastline like this, than they can over a steep or hilly shore.

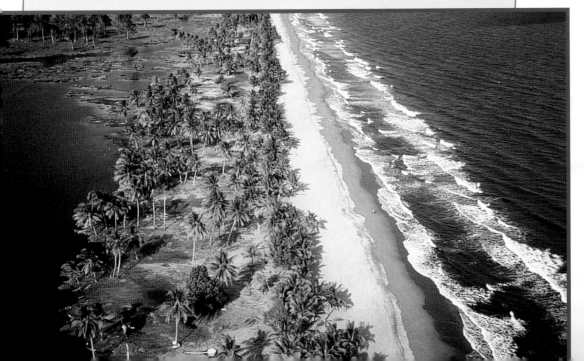

What Happens in a Tsunami?

Tsunamis move very fast. If someone sees one approaching, it is probably too late for him or her to get away from it. Sometimes, though, there are signs that a tsunami is on its way.

Many tsunami survivors describe how the **sea level** drops. Water is suddenly sucked away from the shore, uncovering sand, mud, and reefs on the **seafloor** and leaving fish and boats stranded. The water has moved to fill the space on the ocean floor created by an **earthquake.** Then, the water returns in waves.

"I saw the entire bay suddenly drain of water with a quiet roar." Mark Vanderkam, a survivor of the tsunami that hit Thailand in 2004

Before the first tsunami waves arrive, the sea is sucked back from the shore. This is what it looked like at Galle in Sri Lanka right before the 2004 tsunami hit.

Wave train

As the sea gurgles out from land, there is sometimes a very strong wind. This air is being pushed in front of the speeding tsunami. A big tsunami often comes in a series of waves called a wave train. The time between each wave **crest** may be minutes or even as long as an hour. Between each tsunami crest there is a **trough,** when water is again sucked out to sea. It is as if the water is being pulled by an enormous vacuum cleaner before it rushes back.

The first tsunami wave may not be the worst—the biggest, most dangerous waves in a wave train are often the third and eighth waves to arrive. After a tsunami strikes, it may take days before ocean waves get back to their regular sizes.

The first tsunami wave to break may not cause the most damage. Other, more damaging waves, may arrive later.

13

Destruction

A big tsunami can destroy nearly anything in its path. In an instant, whole areas of homes, farms, and factories may be ruined. Many animals and people may be drowned under several feet of water, or they might be carried as far as half a mile inland. Cars, trains, boats, buses, and shattered buildings and bridges are carried inland at high speed, like missiles. They may crush anything in their way.

An entire coastline may be altered by a tsunami. The seawater may flood large areas of low-lying land, ruining farmers' **crops.** Trees, other plants, and soil are sometimes stripped from the land, and the sucking action of the wave train may shift whole beaches.

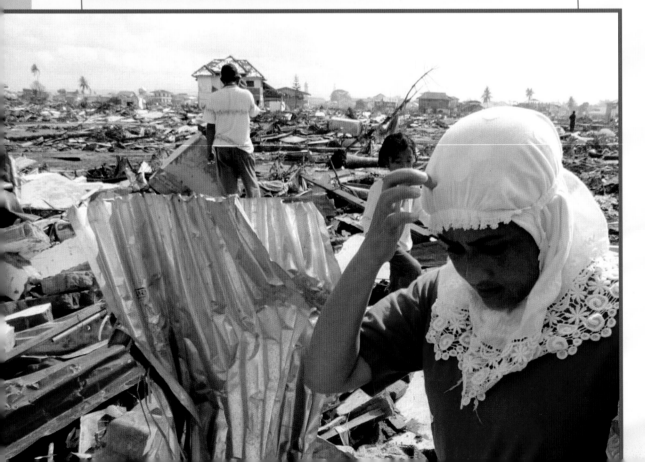

Tsunamis can cause horrific devastation. Whole cities were flattened as a result of the tsunami in late December 2004. This was the city of Banda Aceh in Indonesia.

After the waves

When a tsunami is over, daily life does not return to normal for some time. Many people, such as fishermen with broken boats, cannot earn money because they cannot work. Children may not be able to go to school. There are many health hazards. Drinking water and **sewage** get mixed with seawater when pipes are snapped and **reservoirs** broken. People might drink **polluted** water containing germs that will make them sick. Many people are at risk of **electrocution** from damaged **powerlines.** Sometimes gas that leaks from broken pipes explodes.

When the seawater drains away, massive amounts of **debris** left on land have to be cleared away. Some debris comes from collapsed buildings or trees. Other debris is from the ocean—tsunamis pick up tons of sand, coral, rock, and fish as they approach land.

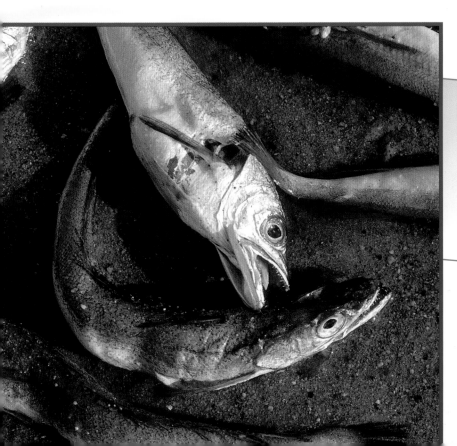

After a tsunami, there is often a terrible odor from piles of rotting fish that the tsunami dumped on land.

The Indian Ocean, 2004

On the morning of December 26, 2004, a huge earthquake shook the seabed off the Indonesian island of Sumatra. A tsunami sped away across the Indian Ocean, traveling at speeds of 300 miles per hour (480 kilometers per hour). The thousands of people who were working, playing, and relaxing on the coasts of eight countries had no idea the tsunami was coming. Their only warning was when the sea suddenly pulled back hundreds of feet from the shore. The first wave caught most people unaware. Indonesia, Sri Lanka, Thailand, and India were hit the hardest and about 250,000 people died.

"A great wave came rushing in to the shore, destroying everything and sweeping away everybody who was in the way. Everyone vanished in a second. The whole town was destroyed, along with people at the bus stop and vehicles on the road."
Deepa, Sri Lankan survivor

The circles on this map show how the earthquake that began near Indonesia caused a tsunami that traveled as far as the coast of eastern Africa.

Damage

Many people were injured and thousands of homes, hotels and businesses were destroyed. Countries as far away as the Maldives and Somalia were affected. The costs of aid, cleaning up, and rebuilding were around $6 billion. The rest of the world was shocked by the scale of the disaster and money flooded in to help victims and restore basic services.

After this disaster, scientists called for a tsunami early warning system around the Indian Ocean, like the one in the Pacific Ocean. The next time a tsunami comes, warning sirens would sound to give people a chance to escape to a safer place.

TSUNAMI FACTS

! The 2004 tsunami took fifteen minutes to reach Indonesia and seven hours to reach Somalia.

! Many victims drowned while picking up fish flung onto the beach by the first waves.

People ran for their lives when the tsunami hit the shore of Koh Raya, Thailand, in 2004.

Who Helps when Tsunamis Happen?

Many people help the victims of tsunamis. Scientists tell coast guards and government officials if there has been an **earthquake** that might start a tsunami. Then fire, police, ambulance services, and the navy are put on alert. Hospitals prepare to treat tsunami victims.

Authorities use radio and TV **broadcasts** to warn people that they may have to **evacuate.** Authorities might also visit people where they live to warn them. If a tsunami is definitely on its way, sirens may be sounded so that people know they must evacuate to a safe place. Most people can travel on their own, but some young, old, or sick people need help evacuating. The police and army usually help organize evacuations.

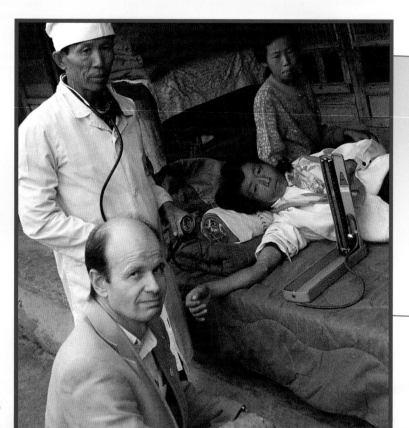

*Local authorities and **charities,** such as the Red Cross, give **first aid** to injured people. They also collect food and water supplies and organize shelter for evacuated people.*

Emergency help

More help is needed if a tsunami happens unexpectedly or if it affects more land than expected. Emergency services find and rescue people who were washed out to sea or trapped in dangerous places such as boats or unsafe buildings. The fire department puts out fires of spilled oil or gas. **Paramedics** and doctors give first aid for injuries such as cuts and broken bones.

In some poorer countries, emergency services may not be able to cope with a tsunami disaster. They will ask for **aid** from other governments and international organizations and charities. Many of these groups may help over a long period, working with local people to rebuild homes and hospitals. In places where farms have been destroyed, they give seeds and **livestock** so people will be able to feed themselves again. They also give new pipes and pumps to provide a safe water supply.

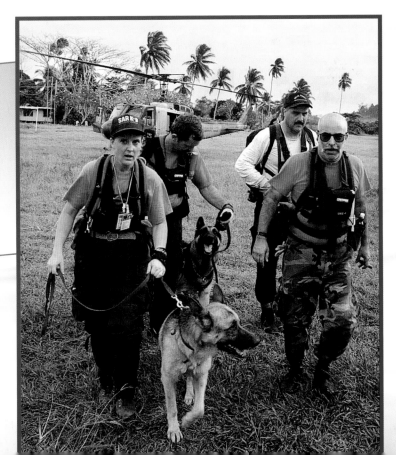

This rescue team has landed in a helicopter. They have search and rescue dogs to help them find people who may be trapped in collapsed buildings.

What to do when a tsunami happens

- People who live or work on the coast should move at least 1 mile (1.6 km) inland or to higher ground.
- People on a boat at deep sea should stay there and not return to land. The farther out to sea over deep water, the lower the wave height.
- People should keep a radio or telephone nearby to listen for further warnings and messages.
- People should never return to a tsunami-hit area until they are told the waves have stopped coming.
- People should stay away from buildings left standing after a tsunami because they might collapse.

People on boats near coasts should head out to sea if they hear a tsunami warning. Boats near the coast will be tossed around and smashed onto the land like toys, like this boat in Banda Ache, Indonesia, in 2004.

Japan, 1993

On July 12, 1993, an **earthquake** struck 12.5 miles (20 km) off the island of Okushiri. The Japanese authorities gave a tsunami warning on radio and TV within five minutes, so many people were able to **evacuate** to higher ground. However, waves 16 to 100 feet (5 to 30 meters) high had already struck Aonae, a fishing village on Okushiri's southern **headland.** More than 200 people were killed by the waves.

The Japan Maritime Safety Agency used helicopters, boats, and divers to find missing people. Heavy cranes and bulldozers were used to clear **debris** that had filled the harbor.

The gymnasium of Aonae Middle School became a temporary shelter for hundreds of people whose homes were destroyed. Their new homes were built farther away from the sea, so any future tsunamis would affect them less.

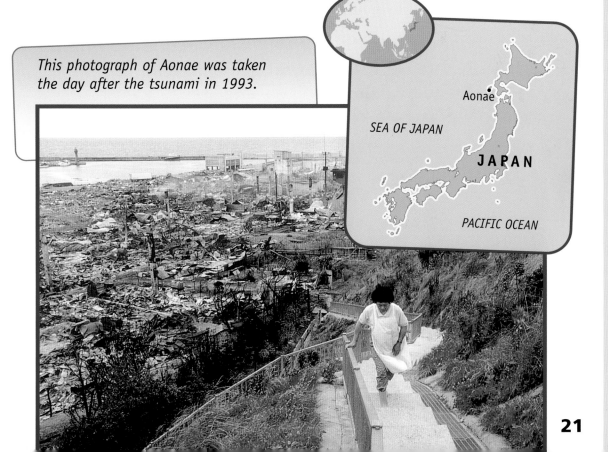

This photograph of Aonae was taken the day after the tsunami in 1993.

Aonae

SEA OF JAPAN

JAPAN

PACIFIC OCEAN

Can Tsunamis Be Predicted?

Scientists around the world work together to predict tsunamis. They use machines called **seismographs** to record when and where **earthquakes** strike and how strong they are. If a big earthquake happens under or near an ocean, scientists warn neighboring countries that there may be a tsunami. However, not every earthquake starts a tsunami, so scientists have developed ways of detecting and tracking tsunamis.

Detecting waves

There is a network of research stations around the Pacific Ocean that measure the heights of tides. Scientists use these stations to notice sudden changes in water level that happen before a tsunami. Scientists from Japan and the United States have laid cables on the ocean floor, near their coasts. Special boxes along the cables sense when a deep tsunami wave passes over them. The boxes send this information via **satellites** to scientists on shore so they know a tsunami is on its way.

The marks on this paper show earth movements recorded by a seismograph. The more the ground shakes, the bigger an earthquake is.

Looking into the future

Many countries use powerful computers to help them **simulate** how tsunamis will affect their coasts. To do this, they prepare electronic maps of coastal places, showing where people live and what the land is like—for example, if it is flat or hilly. They also enter information about earlier tsunamis, such as how far they traveled on flat land and up steeper slopes. Then, they simulate tsunamis of different sizes and speeds hitting these places.

These simulations are vital to figure out the best places to **evacuate** people. Local authorities can then tell people the quickest escape routes if a tsunami approaches. Simulations also show the safest places to build.

These are computer simulations of tsunamis hitting land. They give people an idea of what might happen if a tsunami were to hit their coast.

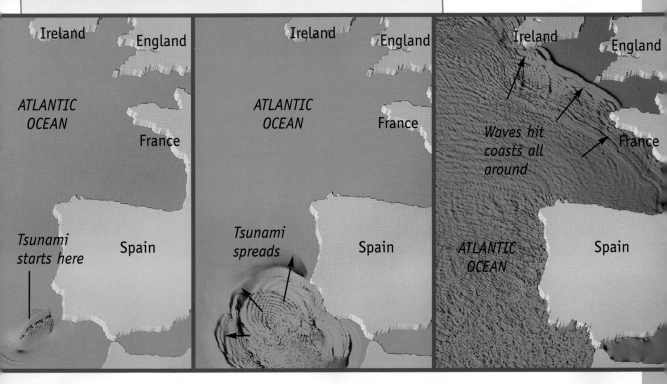

Ireland
England
ATLANTIC OCEAN
France
Tsunami starts here
Spain

Ireland
England
ATLANTIC OCEAN
France
Tsunami spreads
Spain

Ireland
England
Waves hit coasts all around
France
ATLANTIC OCEAN
Spain

Can People Prepare for Tsunamis?

People who live in places threatened by tsunamis must understand the danger they are in. They can then prepare in various ways, from the way they build their houses to knowing how to **evacuate.**

Building for tsunamis

The damage caused by tsunamis can be reduced if buildings are made stronger. For example, most of the repair costs after the Aonae tsunami were spent fixing damaged harbor walls. Since then, new taller and stronger sea walls have been built around parts of Japan. In Hawaii, many office and hotel buildings are now built on stilts—the ground floor is open parking space with rooms above. Water can pass through the open space and not damage the building structure.

This museum in New Zealand is shaped so that waves can move around it. It is also built on rubber feet so waves can move it 2.5 feet (75 cm) without damaging it.

Evacuation plans

It is important for people to know the best way of getting themselves and their family, pets, and farm animals to a safe place. All family members should know how to contact each other or where to meet if they are not all in the same place. They should also know things about where they live and understand evacuation warnings. People should always take evacuation warnings seriously. They should also watch for tsunami signs such as sudden changes in **sea level.**

A tsunami survival kit

If people have to evacuate, they should take these things:

- a **first-aid** kit and any necessary medicines;
- enough food and water for at least three days;
- a flashlight and radio with extra batteries;
- warm clothing, blankets, or sleeping bags;
- money and important papers such as passports and driver's licenses.

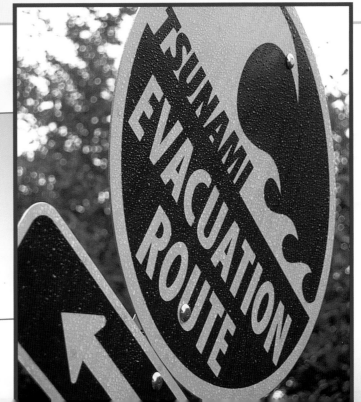

States bordering the Pacific Ocean have put up tsunami signs like this one. They show people which way to go if they hear a tsunami warning on the radio or television.

Papua New Guinea, 1998

In July 1998, an **earthquake** started a giant underwater **landslide** that caused a huge tsunami. It was dusk when three massive waves swept over Arop and other villages around Sissano lagoon in northern Papua New Guinea.

Earthquakes are common in Papua New Guinea because it is near the joint between two of Earth's **plates.** However, most of the local people did not know about tsunamis. A rumble was heard out at sea and many people moved closer to see the water drawing back and then rising above the horizon. Those who could, ran for their lives. The first wave flooded the land and broke up the villagers' flimsy wooden houses. The second wave, which was 32 feet (10 meters) high, swept away everything in front of it. Two whole villages were completely destroyed. Thousands of people were injured or killed, many by being thrown against trees or being hit by floating **debris.** Many of the victims were children.

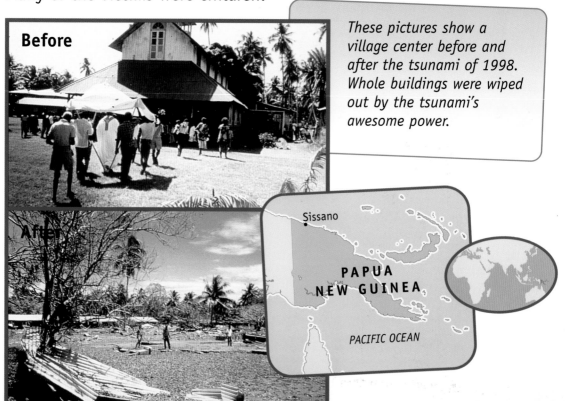

Before

After

These pictures show a village center before and after the tsunami of 1998. Whole buildings were wiped out by the tsunami's awesome power.

Sissano

PAPUA NEW GUINEA

PACIFIC OCEAN